What is a Vision Bo

A vision board is a powerful tool that can help you clarify and manifest your goals and dreams. It is a visual representation of the things you want to achieve, create, or attract in your life. The process of creating a vision board involves gathering images, words, and phrases that represent your desired outcomes and arranging them on a board or piece of paper.

Here are some of the benefits of using a vision board for your wedding:

- Clarify your vision: A vision board helps you visualize your ideal wedding day. By gathering images, words, and other visual cues that represent your dream wedding, you can gain clarity on what you really want for your special day. This can help you make better decisions when it comes to choosing vendors, venues, and other aspects of your wedding.

- Stay focused: Planning a wedding can be overwhelming, and it's easy to get side tracked by small details or competing priorities. A vision board can serve as a reminder of your overall vision for your wedding day and help you stay focused on what's most important.

- Boost your motivation: When you see your vision board every day, it can help you stay motivated and inspired throughout the wedding planning process. You'll be reminded of why you're working so hard to create the wedding of your dreams.

- Attract positive energy: Many people believe that the Law of Attraction can help them manifest their desires. By creating a vision board filled with images and words that represent your ideal wedding day, you can attract positive energy and bring your dreams to life.

First Edition

Here's how to use this Vision Board Clip Art Book:

1. Gather your supplies. Your Vision Board Book, scissors, glue or tape, and a poster board, corkboard or canvas to create your vision board.
2. Set your intention. Take a moment to reflect on what you want to manifest for your wedding. Whatever it is, make sure it's specific and meaningful to you.
3. Flip through your vision board clip art book. Look for images and phrases that represent you.
4. Use scissors to carefully cut out the images and phrases that you want to include on your vision board.
5. Arrange your images on your poster board, corkboard or canvas. Assemble the images in a way that makes sense to you, such as by color scheme or by theme. You can arrange them in a linear fashion or in a more creative collage style.
6. Glue, tape or pin your images in place.
7. Hang your vision board in a place where you'll see it every day. You can also take a picture of it and make it your phone or computer wallpaper.
8. Use the vision board as a reference when making decisions about your wedding. You can refer to it when choosing flowers, selecting a dress, or deciding on decorations.
9. Visualize your intentions. Spend a few minutes each day looking at your vision board and visualizing yourself achieving your dream wedding.
10. Update the vision board as you continue to plan your wedding. You may find new inspirations that you want to add to the board, or you may change your mind about certain elements.

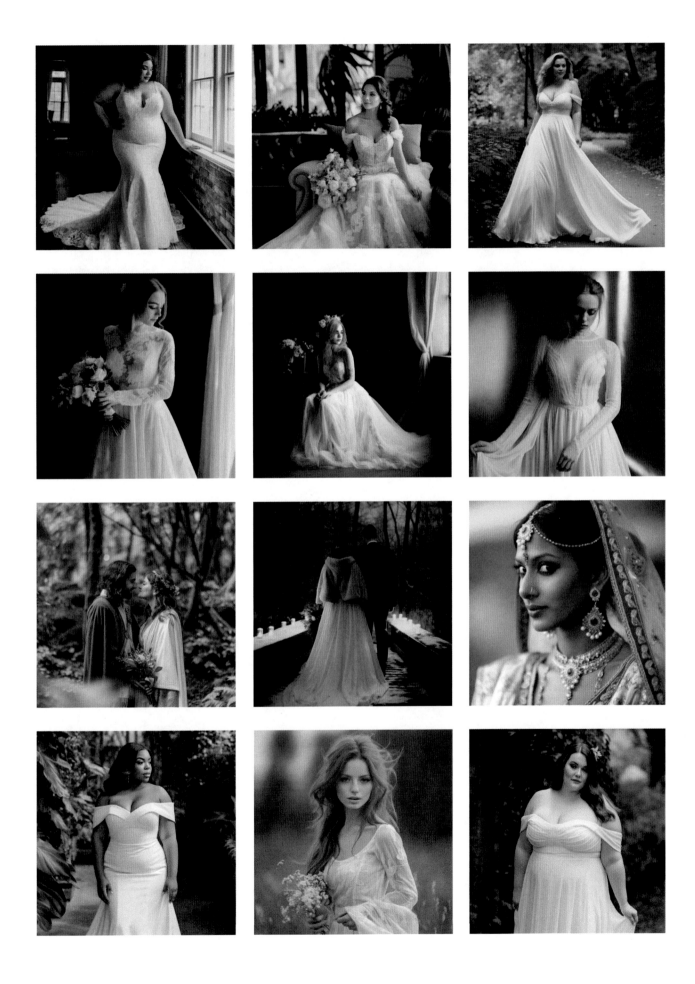

Here Comes
The Bride

Our

Vows

Our

Wedding

Welcome

To have
and to hold

Unplugged
Wedding

A-line

V-neck

Ballgown

Fitted

Boho

Strapless

Sweetheart

Straps

Sleeves

Cape

Veil

Long Train

Black Tie

Destination

Marquee

Elopement

Outdoor

Country

City

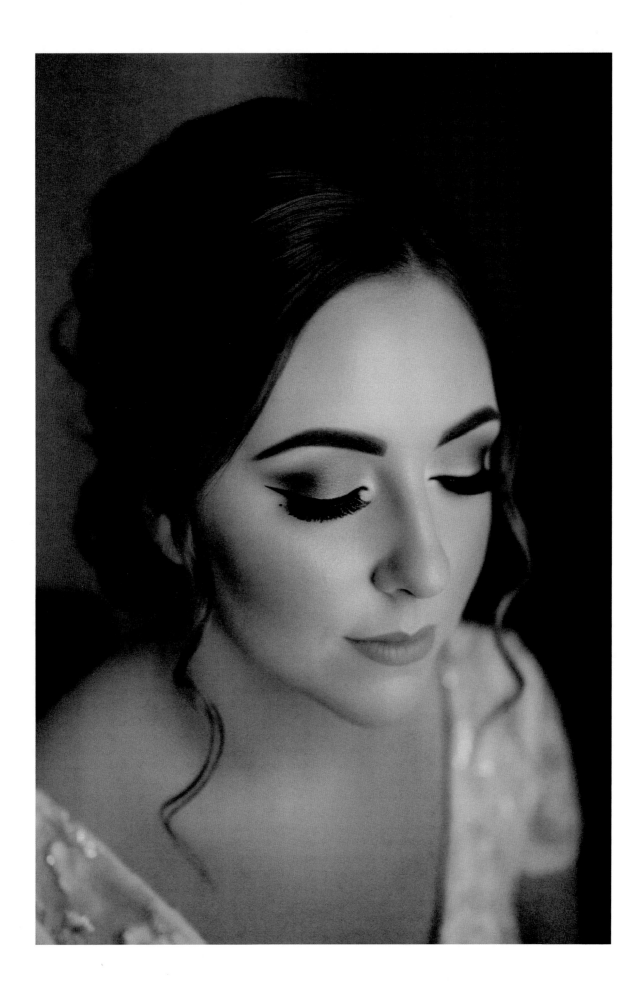

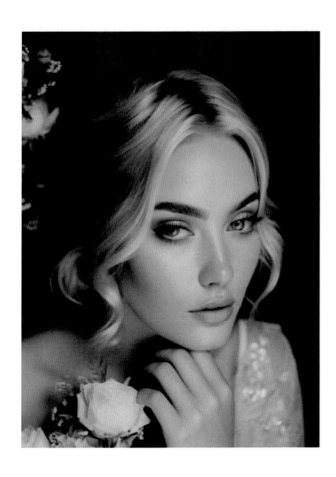

Classic Tuxedos

Modern
Suits

Textured
Fabrics

Bold Colors

Patterns

Statement

Accessories

Art

Gallery

Backyard

Church

Library

Aquarium

Craft brewery

Chateau or castle

Nightclub or lounge

Sports stadium

Theme park

Barn or farm

Treehouse

College or university

Mountain lodge

Botanical garden

Boat or yacht

Cafe and bar

Historic site

Vacation rental

Museum

Restaurant

Beach

Winery or vineyard

Clear

Marquee

Yurt

Clearspan

Tipis

Traditional
Marquees

Slideshow

Sparklers

Photo Booth

Disposable Cameras

Live Band

Horse-Drawn Carriage

DJ

Sunday

Open Bar

Bonfire

Cocktail Bar

Couples Shoe Game

Weekday Wedding

Glow Sticks

Bouquet Toss

Themed Piñata

Champagne Tower

Saturday

Live Painter

Garden games

Zen wedding

Wedding Raffle

Hot Chocolate Bar

Choreographed Dance Routine

Ice Cream Cart

DIY Mimosas

Guest Props

Popcorn Stand

Congratulations on your upcoming wedding! This is an exciting time in your life and we wish you all the best as you plan your special day. May your love continue to grow and flourish as you embark on this new journey together.

If you're not planning a wedding but are using this page as part of your manifestation vision board, we wish you good luck in achieving your goals and dreams. May this be the start of a new chapter in your life filled with success, happiness, and fulfilment.

If you would like a Digital Version of this exact Vision Board feel free to purchase it at **amycatescorner.com**, use the code **visionboardwedding** to receive **15% off.**

Made in the USA
Las Vegas, NV
29 November 2024

12853280R10074